FEB **2 8** 2017

D1123490

Walla Walla
County Libraries

J
641.83
Nikko
2017

COOL Wild Game Recipes

Main Dishes for Beginning Chefs

Parker Nikko

Checkerboard Library

An Imprint of Abdo Publishing
abdopublishing.com

abdopublishing.com

Published by Abdo Publishing, a division of ABDO, PO Box 398166, Minneapolis, Minnesota 55439. Copyright © 2017 by Abdo Consulting Group, Inc. International copyrights reserved in all countries. No part of this book may be reproduced in any form without written permission from the publisher. Checkerboard Library™ is a trademark and logo of Abdo Publishing.

Printed in the United States of America,
North Mankato, Minnesota
102016
012017

THIS BOOK CONTAINS RECYCLED MATERIALS

Design and Production: Mighty Media, Inc.
Series Editor: Liz Salzmann
Photo Credits: Mighty Media, Inc.; Shutterstock
Food Credits: Parker Nikko

The following manufacturers/names appearing in this book are trademarks: Campbell's®, Hunt's®, McCormick®, Old El Paso®, Oster®, Pyrex®, Swanson®

Publisher's Cataloging-in-Publication Data

Names: Nikko, Parker, author.
Title: Cool wild game recipes: main dishes for beginning chefs / by Parker Nikko.
Other titles: Main dishes for beginning chefs
Description: Minneapolis, MN : Abdo Publishing, 2017. | Series: Cool main dish recipes | Includes bibliographical references and index.
Identifiers: LCCN 2016944831 | ISBN 9781680781373 (lib. bdg.) | ISBN 9781680775570 (ebook)
Subjects: LCSH: Cooking--Juvenile literature. | Dinners and dining--Juvenile literature. | Entrees (Cooking)--Juvenile literature. | One-dish meals--Juvenile literature.
Classification: DDC 641.82--dc23
LC record available at http://lccn.loc.gov/2016944831

TO ADULT HELPERS

Get cooking! This is your chance to help a budding chef. Being able to cook meals is a life skill. Learning to cook gives kids new experiences and helps them gain confidence. These recipes are designed to help kids learn how to cook on their own. They may need more assistance on some recipes than others. Be there to offer guidance when they need it. Encourage them to do as much as they can on their own. Make sure to have rules for cleanup. There should always be adult supervision when kids are using sharp utensils or a hot oven or stove.

SAFETY FIRST!

Some recipes call for activities that require caution. If you see these symbols, ask an adult for help.

HOT STUFF!
This recipe requires the use of a stove or oven. Always use pot holders when handling hot objects.

SUPER SHARP!
This recipe includes the use of a sharp utensil, such as a knife or grater.

Contents

Wild About Game!

The main dish is where you start when planning a meal. It's the most important part. Then you choose salads, side dishes, and **desserts** to go with the main dish. Wild game meat comes from animals that were caught living in the wild.

There is a whole world of flavors you can cook up using wild meat. Try **tangy** BBQ duck. Make a spicy **venison** chili. Or cook up tasty **grouse** bites.

Try all of the wild game recipes in this book. Then think of your own ways to cook wild game. The possibilities are endless!

I ♥ WILD GAME

What's not to love about wild game?

Many people like to hunt their own wild game. You can also look for wild game meat at a butcher shop. Check out these tips for preparing the meat.

BRING IT HOME

Have an adult help prepare the meat for cooking. Do not start cooking until the meat has been cleaned. Any metal from bullets or shot in the animal should be taken out. Make sure to cook or freeze any game meat you bring home right away.

TYPES OF WILD GAME

There are many wild animals that are good to eat.

bison	pheasant
duck	rabbit
elk	squirrel
goose	**venison**
grouse	wild boar
moose	wild turkey

KEEP IT CLEAN

Wash your hands before and after touching the meat. Wash any **utensils** that touched raw meat separately from other dishes.

CUTTING THE MEAT

Put uncooked meat on a cutting board. Use a sharp knife to cut it. Always cut away from your fingers.

COOKING BASICS

Ask Permission

- Before you cook, ask **permission** to use the kitchen, cooking tools, and ingredients.

- If you'd like to do something yourself, say so! Just remember to be safe.

- If you would like help, ask for it!

Be Prepared

- Be organized. Knowing where everything is makes cooking safer and more fun!

- Read the directions all the way through before starting a recipe. Follow the directions in order.

- The most important ingredient is preparation! Make sure you have everything you'll need.

Be Smart, Be Safe

- Never cook if you are home alone.

- Always have an adult nearby for hot jobs, such as using the oven or the stove.

- Have an adult around when using a sharp tool, such as a knife or a grater. Always be careful when using these tools!

- Remember to turn pot handles toward the back of the stove. That way you won't accidentally knock the pots over.

Be Neat, Be Clean

- Start with clean hands, clean tools, and a clean work surface.

- Tie back long hair to keep it out of the food.

- Wear comfortable clothing and roll up your sleeves.

- Put extra ingredients and tools away when you're done.

- Wash all the dishes and **utensils**. Clean up your workspace.

COOKING TERMS

BOIL

Boil means to heat liquid until it begins to bubble.

DICE

Dice means to cut something into small squares.

DRAIN

Drain means to remove liquid using a strainer or **colander**.

SIMMER

Simmer means to cook something so it bubbles gently.

SLICE

Slice means to cut something into pieces of the same thickness.

CHOP

Chop means to cut something into small pieces.

CUBE

Cube means to cut something into bite-size squares.

QUARTER

Quarter means to cut something into four equal pieces.

SHRED

Shred means to cut small pieces of something using a grater.

SPRINKLE

Sprinkle means to drop small pieces of something.

STIR

Stir means to mix ingredients together, usually with a large spoon.

INGREDIENTS

Here are some of the
ingredients you will need.

barbecue sauce	beef broth

cheddar cheese	cream of chicken soup	cream of mushroom soup	duck breasts

ground venison	grouse	hard taco shells	kidney beans

pheasant	potatoes	sour cream	taco seasoning

bell peppers

black beans

carrots

celery

egg noodles

fajita seasoning

flour tortillas

goose breasts

lettuce

lime juice

olive oil

onion

tomatoes

tomato paste

vegetable oil

venison roast

TOOLS

Here are some of the tools you will need.

aluminum foil

baking sheet

ladle

large pot

measuring cups

plastic zipper bags

sharp knife

slow cooker

colander

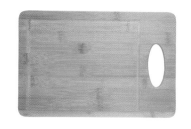

cutting board

electric frying pan

measuring spoons

mixing bowls

mixing spoon

tongs

toothpicks

vegetable peeler

HEARTY
Venison Chili

Kick up your heels and try this chili!

INGREDIENTS

2 tablespoons vegetable oil

1 pound ground venison

2 onions, chopped

¼ tablespoons chili powder

3 6-ounce cans tomato paste

1 26-ounce can beef broth

3 15-ounce cans kidney beans

1 teaspoon cayenne pepper

1 teaspoon coriander

1 tomato, diced

TOOLS

measuring spoons

sharp knife

cutting board

large pot

mixing spoon

pot holders

1 Put the vegetable oil in a large pot. Heat it over medium-high heat for 1 minute. Add the **venison** and onions. Break up the ground venison into small pieces. Stir and cook until the meat is all brown.

2 Add the remaining ingredients.

3 Cook over medium-high heat until the mixture boils. It takes about 15 minutes.

4 Turn the heat to low. Let the chili simmer for 3 hours. Stir it every 30 minutes.

1

2

4

JUICY
Grouse Bites

Take a bite of this bird!

INGREDIENTS

TOOLS

3 grouse breasts
½ cup butter
½ teaspoon salt
½ teaspoon black pepper

measuring spoons
sharp knife
cutting board
electric frying pan
mixing spoon
pot holders
toothpicks

① Cube the **grouse** breasts.

② Put the butter in the electric frying pan. Heat it over medium-high heat until it melts.

③ Add the meat. Stir and cook for 5 minutes, or until the meat is brown.

④ Turn off the heat. Sprinkle the salt and pepper over the meat. Serve with toothpicks.

TIP
For spicy bites, add 1 teaspoon of cayenne pepper while the meat is cooking!

1

2

3

CREAMY
Pheasant Stroganoff

Make a dish that's sure to dazzle!

INGREDIENTS

2 to 3 pheasant breasts
¼ cup butter
1 15-ounce can cream of mushroom soup
1 15-ounce can cream of chicken soup
4 celery stalks, chopped
½ teaspoon salt

½ teaspoon black pepper
1 cup sour cream
8 ounces egg noodles

TOOLS

sharp knife
cutting board
measuring spoons
large pot
measuring cups
mixing spoon
slow cooker

colander
pot holders
ladle
serving bowls

1. Cube the pheasant breasts. Melt the butter in a large pot over medium-high heat.

2. Add the pheasant and ½ cup water. Stir and cook for 10 minutes, or until the meat is browned.

3. Put the pheasant in a slow cooker. Add the soups, celery, salt, and pepper. Stir in the sour cream. Turn the heat to low. Let it cook for 3½ hours.

4. Cook the noodles according to the directions on the package. Drain the noodles.

5. Serve the pheasant mixture over the noodles.

SPICY
Venison Tacos

Spice up taco night!

INGREDIENTS

TOOLS

1 tablespoon vegetable oil
1 pound ground venison
1.25-ounce packet taco seasoning
1 15-ounce can black beans
½ cup chopped onion
8 hard taco shells

1 cup chopped lettuce
½ cup chopped tomatoes
1 cup shredded cheddar cheese

measuring spoons
sharp knife
cutting board
measuring cups
large pot
mixing spoon
pot holders

1. Put the vegetable oil in a large pot. Heat it over medium-high heat for 1 minute. Add the **venison**, taco seasoning, black beans, and onion.

2. Stir and cook for 10 minutes, or until the meat is browned.

3. Put some of the meat mixture in each taco shell.

4. Add lettuce and tomatoes to each taco. Sprinkle cheese on top.

TIP
Try making these tacos with soft tortilla shells!

FIESTY
Goose Fajitas

Have fun with your fajitas!

INGREDIENTS

1 goose breast, cubed
⅓ cup lime juice
2 tablespoons olive oil
1 package fajita seasoning
¼ cup butter
2 tablespoons vegetable oil
1 red bell pepper, sliced

1 orange bell pepper, sliced
1 onion, sliced
5 flour tortillas
½ cup shredded cheddar cheese

TOOLS

sharp knife
cutting board
measuring cups
measuring spoons
large plastic zipper bag
large pot
mixing spoon

pot holders
mixing bowl
tongs

1. Put the goose, lime juice, olive oil, and fajita seasoning in the plastic bag. Shake it to coat the meat. Refrigerate it for 2 hours.

2. Melt the butter in a large pot over medium-high heat.

3. Add the goose. Stir and cook for 10 minutes, or until the meat is browned. Put the meat in a mixing bowl.

4. Put the vegetable oil, peppers, and onions in the pot. Stir and cook for 10 minutes.

5. Put some of the vegetables on a tortilla. Add some of the meat mixture. Sprinkle cheese on top.

6. Repeat step 5 to make more fajitas. Roll them up when you eat them.

3

4

5

PERFECT
Venison Pot Roast

12 carrots, peeled and sliced

8 potatoes, cut into quarters

1 large onion, chopped

3-pound venison roast

salt & black pepper to taste

vegetable peeler
sharp knife
cutting board
slow cooker
pot holders

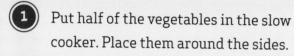

1. Put half of the vegetables in the slow cooker. Place them around the sides.

2. Place the roast on top of the vegetables in the center.

3. Sprinkle salt and pepper on the roast. Put the remaining vegetables on top.

4. Cook on low for 6 hours.

1

2

3

SWEET & TANGY
BBQ Duck Sandwich

Make a meal everyone will be game for!

INGREDIENTS

2 duck breasts,
   skin removed

3 cups barbecue sauce

1 onion, chopped

3 Yukon Gold potatoes, cut
   into 2-inch (5 cm) wedges

2 tablespoons vegetable oil

salt & black pepper to taste

4 hamburger buns

TOOLS

measuring   measuring
   cups   spoons
sharp knife   baking sheet
cutting board   aluminum foil
slow cooker   pot holders
mixing spoon
dinner knife
fork
mixing bowl

1 Put the duck, barbecue sauce, and onion in the slow cooker. Stir to coat the meat and onion with sauce. Cook on high for 3½ hours.

2 Take the duck out of the cooker. Pull the meat apart with a knife and fork. Put the meat back in the cooker. Turn the heat to low.

3 Preheat the oven to 450 degrees. Put the potatoes and oil in a bowl. Add a little salt and pepper. Stir to coat the potatoes.

4 Line a baking sheet with aluminum foil. Spread the potatoes on the baking sheet. Bake for 35 minutes.

5 Put one-fourth of the meat on each bun. Serve the potatoes with the sandwiches.

1

2

3

Conclusion

Explore the world of wild game dishes. What else can you cook up?

Main dishes are fun to make and share! Feel proud of the dishes you prepare. Eat them with your family and friends. Wild game is great for main dishes. Don't stop with wild game. Try other ingredients too!

Glossary

dessert – a sweet food, such as fruit, ice cream, or pastry, served after a meal.

grouse – a type of small, fat game bird that is usually brown with feathers on the legs.

permission – when a person in charge says it's okay to do something.

tangy – having a sharp taste or smell.

utensil – a tool used to prepare or eat food.

venison – meat that comes from a deer.

WEBSITES

To learn more about Cool Main Dishes, visit **booklinks.abdopublishing.com**. These links are routinely monitored and updated to provide the most current information available.

Index